Jezebel's Stronghold: This is the Story of an Actual Man's Journey

Bill Vincent

Published by RWG Publishing, 2022.

While every precaution has been taken in the preparation of this book, the publisher assumes no responsibility for errors or omissions, or for damages resulting from the use of the information contained herein.

JEZEBEL'S STRONGHOLD: THIS IS THE STORY OF AN ACTUAL MAN'S JOURNEY

First edition. March 4, 2022.

Copyright © 2022 Bill Vincent.

Written by Bill Vincent.

Also by Bill Vincent

Building a Prototype Church: Divine Strategies Released
Experience God's Love: By Revival Waves of Glory School of the Supernatural
Glory: Expanding God's Presence
Glory: Increasing God's Presence
Glory: Kingdom Presence of God
Glory: Pursuing God's Presence
Glory: Revival Presence of God
Rapture Revelations: Jesus Is Coming
The Prototype Church: Heaven's Strategies for Today's Church
The Secret Place of God's Power
Transitioning Into a Prototype Church: New Church Arising
Spiritual Warfare Made Simple
Aligning With God's Promises
A Closer Relationship With God
Armed for Battle: Spiritual Warfare Battle Commands
Breakthrough of Spiritual Strongholds
Desperate for God's Presence: Understanding Supernatural Atmospheres
Destroying the Jezebel Spirit: How to Overcome the Spirit Before It Destroys You!
Discerning Your Call of God

Glory: Expanding God's Presence: Discover How to Manifest God's Glory

Glory: Kingdom Presence Of God: Secrets to Becoming Ambassadors of Christ

Satan's Open Doors: Access Denied

Spiritual Warfare: The Complete Collection

The War for Spiritual Battles: Identify Satan's Strategies

Understanding Heaven's Court System: Explosive Life Changing Secrets

A Godly Shaking: Don't Create Waves

Faith: A Connection of God's Power

Global Warning: Prophetic Details Revealed

Overcoming Obstacles

Spiritual Leadership: Kingdom Foundation Principles

Glory: Revival Presence of God: Discover How to Release Revival Glory

Increasing Your Prophetic Gift: Developing a Pure Prophetic Flow

Millions of Churches: Why Is the World Going to Hell?

The Supernatural Realm: Discover Heaven's Secrets

The Unsearchable Riches of Christ: Chosen to be Sons of God

Deep Hunger: God Will Change Your Appetite Toward Him

Defeating the Demonic Realm

Glory: Increasing God's Presence: Discover New Waves of God's Glory

Growing In the Prophetic: Developing a Prophetic Voice

Healing After Divorce: Grace, Mercy and Remarriage

Love is Waiting

Awakening of Miracles: Personal Testimonies of God's Healing Power

Deception and Consequences Revealed: You Shall Know the Truth and the Truth Shall Set You Free
Overcoming the Power of Lust
Are You a Follower of Christ: Discover True Salvation
Cover Up and Save Yourself: Revealing Sexy is Not Sexy
Heaven's Court System: Bringing Justice for All
The Angry Fighter's Story: Harness the Fire Within
The Wrestler: The Pursuit of a Dream
Beginning the Courts of Heaven: Understanding the Basics
Breaking Curses: Legal Rights in the Courts of Heaven
Writing and Publishing a Book: Secrets of a Christian Author
How to Write a Book: Step by Step Guide
The Anointing: Fresh Oil of God's Presence
Spiritual Leadership: Kingdom Foundation Principles Second Edition
The Courts of Heaven: How to Present Your Case
The Jezebel Spirit: Tactics of Jezebel's Control
Heaven's Angels: The Nature and Ranking of Angels
Don't Know What to Do?: Discover Promotion in the Wilderness
Word of the Lord: Prophetic Word for 2020
The Coronavirus Prophecy
Increase Your Anointing: Discover the Supernatural
Apostolic Breakthrough: Birthing God's Purposes
The Healing Power of God: Releasing the Power of the Holy Spirit
The Secret Place of God's Power: Revelations of God's Word
The Rapture: Details of the Second Coming of Christ
Increase of Revelation and Restoration: Reveal, Recover & Restore

Restoration of the Soul: The Presence of God Changes Everything

Building a Prototype Church: The Church is in a Season of Profound of Change

Keys to Receiving Your Miracle: Miracles Happen Today

The Resurrection Power of God: Great Exploits of God

Transitioning to the Prototype Church: The Church is in a Season of Profound of Transition

Waves of Revival: Expect the Unexpected

The Stronghold of Jezebel: A True Story of a Man's Journey

Glory: Pursuing God's Presence: Revealing Secrets

Like a Mighty Rushing Wind

Steps to Revival

Supernatural Power

The Goodness of God

The Secret to Spiritual Strength

The Glorious Church's Birth: Understanding God's Plan For Our Lives

God's Presence Has a Profound Impact On Us

Spiritual Battles of the Mind: When All Hell Breaks Loose, Heaven Sends Help

A Godly Shaking Coming to the Church: Churches are Being Rerouted

Relationship with God in a New Way

The Spirit of God's Anointing: Using the Holy Spirit's Power in You

The Magnificent Church: God's Power Is Being Manifested

Miracles Are Awakened: Today is a Day of Miracles

Prepared to Fight: The Battle of Deliverance

The Journey of a Faithful: Adhering to the teachings of Jesus Christ

Ascension to the Top of Spiritual Mountains: Putting an End to Pain Cycles

After Divorce Recovery: When I Think of Grace, I Think of Mercy and Remarriage

A Greater Sense of God's Presence: Learn How to Make God's Glory Visible

Do Not Allow the Enemy to Steal: To a Crown of Righteousness, a Crown of Thorns

There Are Countless Churches: What is the Cause of Global Doom?

Creating a Model Church: The Church is Undergoing Considerable Upheaval

Developing Your Prophetic Ability: Creating a Flow of Pure Prophetic Intent

Christ's Limitless Riches Are Unsearchable: God Has Chosen Us to Be His Sons

Faith is a Link Between God's Might and Ours

Increasing the Presence of God: The Revival of the End-Times Is Approaching

Getting a Prophecy for Yourself: Unlocking Your Prophecies with Prophetic Keys

Getting Rid of the Jezebel Spirit: Before the Spirit Destroys You, Here's How to Overcome It!

Getting to Know Heaven's Court System: Secrets That Will Change Your Life

God's Resurrected Presence: Revival Glory is Being Released

God's Presence In His Kingdom: Secrets to Becoming Christ's Ambassadors

God's Healing Ability: The Holy Spirit's Power is Being Released

God's Power of Resurrection: God's Great Exploits

Heaven's Supreme Court: Providing Equal Justice for All
Increasing God's Presence in Our Lives: God's Glory Has Reached New Heights
Jezebel's Stronghold: This is the Story of an Actual Man's Journey
Making the Shift to the Model Church: The Church Is In the Midst of a Major Shift
Overcoming Lust's Influence: The Way to Victory
Pursuing God's Presence: Disclosing Information
The Plan to Take Over America: Restoring, We the People and the Power of God
Revelation and Restoration Are Increasing: The Process That Reveals, Recovers, and Restores
Burn In the Presence of the Lord
Revival Tidal Waves: Be Prepared for the Unexpected
Taking down the Demonic Realm: Curses and Revelations of Demonic Spirits
The Apocalypse: Details about Christ's Second Coming
The Hidden Resource of God's Power
The Open Doors of Satan: Access is Restricted
The Secrets to Getting Your Miracle
The Truth About Deception and Its Consequences
The Universal World: Discover the Mysteries of Heaven
Warning to the World: Details of Prophecies Have Been Revealed
Wonders and Significance: God's Glory in New Waves
Word of the Lord
Why Is There No Lasting Revival: It's Time For the Next Move of God
A Double New Beginning: A Prophetic Word, the Best Is Yet to Come

Your Most Productive Season Ever: The Anointing to Get Things Done
Break Free From Prison: No More Bondage for the Saints
Breaking Strongholds: Taking Steps to Freedom
Carrying the Glory of God: Igniting the End Time Revival
Breakthrough Over the Enemies Attack on Resources: An Angel Called Breakthrough
Days of Breakthrough: Your Time is Now
Empowered For the Unprecedented: Extraordinary Days Ahead
The Ultimate Guide to Self-Publishing: How to Write, Publish, and Promote Your Book for Free
The Art of Writing: A Comprehensive Guide to Crafting Your Masterpiece
The Non-Fiction Writer's Guide: Mastering Engaging Narratives
Spiritual Leadership (Large Print Edition): Kingdom Foundation Principles
Desperate for God's Presence (Large Print Edition): Understanding Supernatural Atmospheres
From Writer to Marketer: How to Successfully Promote Your Self-Published Book
Unleashing Your Inner Author: A Step-by-Step Guide to Crafting Your Own Bestseller
Becoming a YouTube Sensation: A Guide to Success

Watch for more at https://revivalwavesofgloryministries.com/.

Table of Contents

Introduction 1
The Spirit of Jezebel 3
Initially, there was nothing. 17
The Reign of Jezebel has come to an end 25
Jezebel's characteristics are as follows 31
Jezebel employs the practice of witchcraft 33

Introduction

A book that God has been impressing upon me for quite some time is being published. Both men and women, I believe, have had first-hand experience with a demonic spirit known as Jezebel. I'm not simply referring to a remote spirit in the Church; I'm referring to a spirit who is genuinely married to this vile spirit.

This is a factual story about my own personal experiences. I was actually married to a woman who had a Jezebel spirit in her. I'll tell you the story, but I'll leave out the names of the characters because we're not dealing with flesh and blood here, but rather with Principalities and Powers of evil in high places.

STARTING WITH A CHAPTER that provides some scriptural support for the spirit of Jezebel and the traits of this spirit, I will lay the groundwork for the rest of the book. Then I'll create the story, using as many, if not all, of the qualities of the Jezebel spirit as I can find in my research.

While I understand that some people will become enraged and strike out at me, I ask you not to pass judgment until you have walked a mile in my shoes. This book will be divisive, and if you know me at all, you know that I thrive in the midst of controversy. It has been approximately eighteen months since

I parted ways with Jezebel. I'm not writing this to vent or to put someone else down in any way. This book is intended to be of assistance to someone if they are in the process of being swallowed by a spirit and need to cut them off in order to survive.

The Spirit of Jezebel

The purpose of this Chapter is to provide some scriptural support for the Jezebel Spirit as well as some of its traits. The real Prophets of God have been restored to their rightful places. At the same time, there has been an increase in the number of false prophets, Jezebel, and witchcraft practitioners. The enemy has been assigned the task of assassinating God's real Prophets. We are going to begin breaking every assignment and casting a curse against God's real Prophets as soon as possible.

(Amos 3:7) As a matter of fact, the Lord GOD will not do anything, but he will reveal his secret to his servants, the prophets.

Only his prophetic slaves are privy to his innermost thoughts and plans, though. They maintain a rigorous connection with him, and he provides them with glimpses of what is to come. Such mysteries of God are revealed to them in order that they may inform the people; that, through repentance and conversion, they may avoid the evil; and that, by walking closely with God, they may ensure the continuation of his favor with the people.

First and foremost, let us consider false Prophets.

"Not everyone who says 'Lord, Lord' is a member of God's family."

Matthew 7:15-18 is a biblical passage. Be on the lookout for false prophets who appear to you in sheep's clothes but are really ravening wolves on the inside. You will recognize them by the rewards of their labor. Do men collect grapes from thorns, or figs from thistles, or something else? In the same way, every good tree bears excellent fruit, whilst every corrupt tree bears evil fruit, and vice versa. A good tree cannot bear wicked fruit, and a corrupt tree cannot bear fruit that is beneficial to the environment.

Jeremiah 23:25-27 is a passage from the Old Testament. That prophecy, which is in my name, says, "I have dreamed, I have dreamed," and I have heard what the prophets have spoken about it. How long will this continue to be in the hearts of prophets who prophesy deception? Yes, they are prophets of their own deception; they believe that by telling their dreams to everyone they know, they will cause my people to lose my name, just as their fathers had forgotten my name for Baal, and so will they cause my people to forget my name.

False prophets who employ a witchcraft spirit, for example.

The prophet Jeremiah 27:9 and 10 Do not listen to your prophets, nor to your diviners, nor to your dreamers, nor to your enchanters, nor to your sorcerers who speak to you, saying, "Ye shall not serve the king of Babylon." For they prophesy a lie to you, that I should drive you from your land, and that you would perish as a result of your actions.

Matthew 24:11 (KJV) And there will be many false prophets who will spring up and deceive many people.

Matthew 24:24 (KJV) For there will arise fake Christs and false prophets, and they will perform great shows and wonders,

JEZEBEL'S STRONGHOLD: THIS IS THE STORY OF AN ACTUAL MAN'S JOURNEY

to such an extent that, if it were possible, they will deceive the very elect who have believed the truth.

Mark 13:22 is a Bible verse that describes a relationship between two people. For fake Christs and false prophets will arise, and they will perform miracles and perform signs in order to lure, if at all possible, even the elect.

Many people would prefer to hear from a fictitious Prophet....

2 Timothy 4:2-4 (NASB) Prophesy the word; be punctual in season and out of season; reprove, admonish, and exhort with all patience and doctrine. For the time will come when they will not endure sound doctrine, but will load instructors upon themselves according to their own lusts, and their ears will become itchy as a result; and they will turn aside their ears from the truth and will be converted to lies as a result of this.

As a result, my son, be strong in the grace that is available through Christ Jesus. In addition, the things that you have heard about me from numerous witnesses, you should commit to trustworthy men who will be able to educate others as well. As a good soldier of Jesus Christ, you must consequently persevere in the face of opposition.

Every one of the False Prophets appears to have a problem with Covetousness.

Covetousness is defined as 1. a strong or inordinate desire to obtain and possess some perceived good; it is usually used negatively, and is related to an excessive desire for wealth or avarice.

Covetousness is a feeling that arises from the heart. Inflict pain on your members and encourage covetousness, which is idolatry.

2. A strong urge or a sense of impatience

True Prophets live in peace with one another and with the other True Prophets of God.

Here are a few characteristics of a fake prophet....... They may exhibit some or all of the features listed above.

They have a spirit of deception.

They take use of the Word for their own gain.

They are in open defiance of authorities.

They have a strong sense of authority.

They speak in a way that the pastors find pleasing. True prophets are simply required to speak what has been given to them by the Holy Spirit.

They are primarily interested on money... (much like taking offerings for miracles.) There are people who will accept offerings and misinterpret scripture in order to obtain financial gain.

Let's have a look at Jezebel. They may exhibit some or all of the qualities listed above.

These individuals are on a mission to eliminate the true prophets and prevent them from assuming their proper position within the Church. (They despise the true prophet because they are afraid of being exposed.)

They are attempting to ascertain the position of the authentic prophet.

They agitate and manipulate the situation.

They play an important role in the establishment of false prophets.

They rise up in revolt....

This is the sin of witchcraft, and it is a serious one.

JEZEBEL'S STRONGHOLD: THIS IS THE STORY OF AN ACTUAL MAN'S JOURNEY

They are motivated by hatred, vengeance, and murder. (Destroying someone's reputation is included among the many definitions of murder.) That is exactly what Jezebel will attempt to do to people who have seen through their deception.

They have a spirit of deception.

Jezebel can take the form of either a guy or a woman.

They play games with their partner and manipulate him or her.

If Jezebel is not already in a position of leadership, they will always strive to get promoted to that position.

Jezebel employs the practice of witchcraft.

They have a strong sense of authority.

They do not act in accordance with what is right in God's eyes, but rather according to what is right in their own eyes.

They accuse Authentic Prophets of not delivering the entire true Word of the Lord in its entirety.

Jezebel possesses a seductive spirit, and she infects the body of Christ in the same way that a virus infects a computer.

They are looking to be the focus of worship and/or the center of attention in their community.

They are strict in their demands for compliance to their every command.

Jezebel prophesies through the assistance of familiar spirits.

They are full of intimidation, pride, and hatred, and they refuse to submit (despite the fact that they pretend to be submitting). They also sow strife.

They are a threat to authority.

They follow a religious belief system (appears to be loyal, faithful, but only to accomplish its purpose.)

They are unable to admit they were incorrect. It's always the fault of someone else.

Humility that isn't real

Considers themselves to be of significance.

Continue reading to learn more about Witchcraft and the traits of witchcraft that may exist within the Church.

Sorcery

With the assistance of malevolent spirits, you can perform divination.

Witchcraft has always had the ability to exert control.

Nothing that Jesus has paid for us is upheld by this doctrine.

Witchcraft and the presence of a Controlling Spirit are synonymous.

It is possible that a believer's sense of independence (or rebelliousness against authority) has been corrupted by the spirit of witchcraft.

There are believers who have taken advantage of their liberty in Christ and have utilized that freedom as a defense in times of revolt. It everything boils down to one's inner state of mind.

We must have a heartfelt desire to obey God's Word and to live in freedom without revolting against it.

We must be able to scrutinize our own minds and intentions and make accurate judgments. Putting our trust in someone who has insight of the Spirit of the Lord can help us to achieve our goals.

In the false Prophet and Jezebel, the witchcraft spirit is active, and this has caused pastors to be fearful of the actual Prophets.

JEZEBEL'S STRONGHOLD: THIS IS THE STORY OF AN ACTUAL MAN'S JOURNEY

When it comes to dealing with the False Prophet, Jezebel, and witchcraft, we have to be very careful... We're dealing with the demon Baal.

Here are some things to think about when it comes to Baal: Baal is a false god, to begin with.

This false deity provides a false sense of security and wealth before destroying anybody who chooses to serve him.

Baal is an Arabic name that loosely translates as "The Storm God."

Baal is a god of the weather and fertility.

This was shown to me by God. When dealing with the false god Baal, you are dealing with a swarming thick spirit that is present in the environment at the time of the encounter.

Expect some dark emotions in the spirit, as well as tumultuous spiritual seasons, in the coming months.

Baal is also referred to as the deity of wealth.

Jezebel's death is recorded in 2 Kings 9:33. And he commanded, "Throw her on the ground." In response, they flung her to the ground, and part of her blood was strewn on the wall as well as the horses, and he trampled her underfoot.

Jezebel will not be spared.

BAAL, WITCHCRAFT, FALSE prophets, and Jezebel all have a large number of spirits gathered together to aid them in their evil destructive methods.

2 Kings 10:26-28 (King James Version) And they carried the pictures of Baal out of the house of Baal and set them ablaze. And they demolished the figure of Baal, as well as the Baal's

dwelling, which is still in use as a draught house to this day. As a result, Jehu drove Baal from the land of Israel.

It takes the anointing of God to bring down Ahab, Jezebel, False Prophets, Witchcraft, and Baal from their positions of power.

We must not allow these Spirits to infiltrate and take control of our congregations and our lives.

2 Thessalonians 2:9-12 (New International Version) That is to say, even him, whose coming is in accordance with Satan's working, complete with all power and miracles, and deceptive marvels, and complete with all deceivableness of unrighteousness in those who perish, because they did not receive the love of the truth, that they might be saved. And it is for this reason that God will send them severe delusion, so that they will accept a lie: so that all of those who did not believe the truth, but took pleasure in unrighteousness, will be condemned together.

Micah 5:11-13 is a biblical passage. And I will cut off thy land's cities from the rest of the world, and I will demolish all of thy strongholds; and I will take witchcraft out of thine hands, and thou shalt have no more soothsayers. In addition, I will take away thy graven images and thy standing images from within the midst of you; you are no longer permitted to worship the labor of thine own hands.

A jezebel spirit will be dispatched by the devil whenever a person or church begins to prophesy, in an attempt to derail the prophetic process. If a Church is pursuing the supernatural, a spirit will attempt to enter and ruin what God is accomplishing in the church.

JEZEBEL'S STRONGHOLD: THIS IS THE STORY OF AN ACTUAL MAN'S JOURNEY

According to the Old Testament, Jezebel was a woman who encouraged the worship of idols.... When it comes to women, they are often considered nasty and cunning....

According to the Bible, the wicked woman who married Ahab, the king of Israel, was a.... Any lady who is considered to be shameless and wicked.

This energy, I believe, may be felt by women, men, or even a couple at the same time. Here are a few things that Jezebel is well-known for:

Jezebel assassinated God's prophets, worshipped Baal, engaged in sexual immorality such as orgies, controlled Ahab (her husband) by sending threatening letters to prophets, exercising control via fear and deception, and wrote letters in her husband's name, among other things.

We have been given the authority to cast out devils.

(Luke 10:17) As a result, the seventy returned with a joyful heart, proclaiming, "Lord, even the devils are subservient to us by thy name."

Matthew 16:17 As a result, Jesus responded by saying to him, "Blessed art thou, Simon Barjona," for it was not flesh and blood that revealed it to him, but rather my Father who is in heaven.

Scripture Reference: Revelation 2:20-22 In spite of this, I have a few grievances against thee, primarily because thou permitst that woman Jezebel, who claims to be a prophetess, to educate and seduce my servants into immorality and the consumption of goods consecrated to idols. And I gave her time to repent of her fornication; but, she did not repent of her fornication. If she does not repent of her sins, I will toss her into a bed, and those who commit adultery with her will suffer greatly as a result of their actions.

The spirit of Jezebel will want to exert control.

Jezebel can take the form of either a guy or a woman. This spirit is primarily derived from the act of controlling or being controlled.

People are controlled by this Spirit by intimidation and terror. It aspires to ascend to positions of authority.

Couples may even experience the presence of the spirit. Initial impressions are that they are fantastic, devoted individuals that attend all meetings, work tirelessly to completely support the mission, and volunteer their time and services.

They express their support with their mouths, but their hearts are far away from you and your cause. After a period, they begin to speak with members of the church who have positions of authority (I am concerned about the Pastors, the leaders, the finances, and the way things are done).

Jezebel is a spirit with two distinct personalities.

The name Jezebel is derived from two separate words. Friend or buddy on one side, killer on the other, that is how they are described in the Old Testament.

On the other hand, it has two words in the New Testament: chaste (which means: not engaging in unlawful sexual activity; virtuous.... Sexually abstinent; celibate.... Pure, decent, or modest in nature, behavior, etc.) and continually sinful (which means: not engaging in unlawful sexual activity; virtuous.... Sexually abstinent; celibate....

When you have a bad feeling, the majority of individuals you ask will tell you that you are wrong. (NOT THEM, THOUGH! THEY ARE SUCH NICE PEOPLE) The secret weapon of the Jezebel spirit is that when faced, they will deny

JEZEBEL'S STRONGHOLD: THIS IS THE STORY OF AN ACTUAL MAN'S JOURNEY

everything and make you believe that something is wrong with you.

Jezebel is unyielding in the face of adversity.

The term Jezebel can also refer to someone who refuses to cohabit with others unless they are in complete control of the situation.

A. Jezebel is attracted to those who are weak.

Ahab was an ineffective leader. If a person with a Jezebel Spirit marries, they become the head of household.

(Revelations 2:20) In spite of this, I have a few grievances against thee, primarily because thou permitst that woman Jezebel, who claims to be a prophetess, to educate and seduce my servants into immorality and the consumption of goods consecrated to idols.

God did not address her; she addressed herself.

Signs and symptoms of a Jezebel

You are afraid to spend money, despite the fact that you are the one in charge.

You are hesitant to talk to a leader, despite the fact that people are grumbling about them and that they are churning through employees like they are going out of fashion. The takeovers are taking place in your leadership, and the same person has taken over all of the responsibilities.

You will not be able to do anything on the spur of the moment without first seeking this person's approval.

The ministry, your spouse, or maybe life itself has become a source of discouragement and depression for you, and you are contemplating quitting.

Dislike for authority is one of the characteristics of a Jezebel spirit.

Jezebel enjoys being praised, but she is praised by no one.

Control

If they are submissive, they are merely doing it to gain control over the situation. They can never be pleased; offer them one area and they will demand more and more until they are completely satisfied. It has the effect of a medicine on them. They want to have complete control over the funds. Whoever has authority over the finances also has control over the vision.

They have complete control over the flow of the Holy Spirit. When the Jezebel Spirit is present in the home, the righteous, peace, and joy that should be present are replaced with confusion, discord, and a striving spirit, which is contrary to what should be there. When they depart, tithes have been collected, souls have returned, and God is moving mightily.

It instills a desire to succeed.

Ministers who have a striving spirit are more likely to burn out. It has the potential to drive leaders to strive for more money and more followers, which can only lead to disaster.

Elijah was pushed to the brink of insanity.

It invites allegations and condemnation, and it makes the leader desire to commit suicide as a result.

Has a lust-inspiring spirit that they channel through them.

Jezebel was a seductive woman who exploited her sensuality to influence and manipulate others.

How did it get into the building in the first place?

Exodus 20:5 is a verse from the Bible that describes a relationship between a man and a woman. Because I, the LORD thy God, am a vengeful God, visiting the iniquity of the fathers upon the children to the third and fourth generation of those

JEZEBEL'S STRONGHOLD: THIS IS THE STORY OF AN ACTUAL MAN'S JOURNEY

who hate me, thou shalt not bow down thyself to them or serve them. Rather, thou shalt not serve them.

What is the best way to free a person?

(John 20:23) They are remitted to the person who committed the offense, and they are retained by the one who committed the sin against them.

IT IS TRUE THAT IF you pardon the crimes of any, they are forgiven; nevertheless, if you maintain the sins of any, they are retained.)

As a result, if you repent of sins committed by your parents or grandparents and turn away from their sins, you must also repent of your own sins; if you fail to do so, you are deemed to have kept your own sins.

Galatians 3:13 We have been redeemed by Christ, who took on the curse of the law on our behalf: for it is stated, "Cursed is everyone who hangeth on a tree:"

REPENTANCE

What is the best way to deliver your Church?

For speaking the Word of the Lord, Jezebel despises those who are called Prophets. It despises prayer because it believes that prayer ties it.

There are four steps to winning.

Confrontation on a personal level

Matthew 18:15 For further guidance, should your brother do an act of vengeance against thee, go and confess it to him in private between thee and him alone. If he listens to you, you have won your brother.

Bring witnesses to the confrontation with you.

Matthew 18:16 But if he refuses to listen to you, take one or two more witnesses with you so that every statement can be proven by the testimony of two or three witnesses.

Take it to the local church or temple.

Matthew 18:17 And if he refuses to listen to them, inform the church; nevertheless, if he refuses to listen to the church, he shall be considered a heathen man and a publican by thee.

God will uphold the decision in the hereafter.

Matthew 18:18 Everything that you bind on earth will be bound in heaven, and everything that you free on earth will be loosed in heaven, I assure you of this truth.

Initially, there was nothing.

I grew up in an environment where things were difficult. When the relationship began, I was just seventeen years old. I don't believe she was possessed by the spirit of Jezebel at the time, but I'm sure it wasn't long until she was. I had only recently been converted, and the woman who would become my wife had been impacted by the spirit of Jezebel; in fact, she played a significant role in my salvation.

I was in such a state of appreciation for this woman's assistance in bringing me out of a life of drugs and drink that I had a negative attitude towards her. I recall that I was walking home from work when I began to experience these feelings, which I now believe were caused by a seducing spirit. When I had those sentiments, I even bound the enemy that day, and she persuaded me that the sensations were from God, despite the fact that she was married to another guy at the time of the feelings. Before getting married, the couple had been together for five to six years. During that period, she divorced her husband, and the woman did assist me in obtaining employment and establishing some kind of a life.

There were times when the influence of the Jezebel spirit seemed to be powerful, and other times when it didn't appear to be present at all. In the event that I came to believe that I was being controlled by her, the spirit would go into hibernation.

You should be aware that, aside from the spirit of Jezebel that was in her, I dealt with a variety of other wicked spirits throughout my early years and even later years of my career. I was brought up in a world of deception, lust, and robbing in order to go ahead. The important thing for you to understand is that I'm exposing myself in order to let people know that God has worked with me and made me into a revival preacher who preaches with healing, signs and wonders, and who preaches with healing, miracles, and signs and wonders. It comes after a long series of setbacks and setbacks. There was nothing quite like the spirit of Jezebel that I had to deal with during my time as a man of God. It was the most powerful thing I had to deal with.

Have you ever heard the expression "what doesn't kill us makes us stronger"? In fact, I have been used to deliver over a thousand people, and I am certain that this is due to the Holy Spirit's work in me. He has continued to teach me throughout much of my life. See, I had been married to Jezebel for thirteen years and had been in a relationship with her for a total of nineteen years at the time of this writing. This woman, who possessed the spirit of Jezebel, had been a part of my life for almost as long as Jesus had been a part of mine. To get where I am now, I've had to be knocked down, humiliated in front of others, and to feel defeated while also being rewarded by God in the process. Despite the fact that I have been engaged in a number of ongoing struggles, God has transformed me into a man of God.

This Is the Day of the Wedding

After being in a relationship for several years, we decided to tie the knot. The ceremony took place in a small home, and it was a private affair. We got married, and I realized that it was strange not to have any relatives or friends, but she persuaded

JEZEBEL'S STRONGHOLD: THIS IS THE STORY OF AN ACTUAL MAN'S JOURNEY

me that it was good this time. Another thing that perplexed me was the fact that we never consummated the marriage, which is something that most couples do on their wedding day.

This marriage was always going to be legally binding on me. I'd constantly have a new restricted region in my life to contend with. Understand that I made my fair share of heinous errors, yet I was continually criticized. Being married to someone who possesses a Jezebel spirit is similar to being raised by a stern mother who harbors bad intentions. Soon after we were married, she insisted on us keeping our relationship a secret from her family, and if she saw someone she recognized, she pretended she didn't know who I was.

It took a few of years before she began to recognize me as her husband in any meaningful way. I now realize that this was due to the fact that God has truly poured out His anointing on my life. My prophetic and preaching abilities grew as the anointing of the Holy Spirit grew stronger and stronger. This was the time when the evil spirit Jezebel made a big appearance in her life for the first time. When the call of a Prophet of God was placed on my life, she grew in strength.

This was not a typical marriage in any sense of the word. Despite being married for thirteen years, there has been no sexual activity for more than ten of those years.

The Ministry of Health and Human Services

After several years of marriage, we began to travel for ministry, which eventually led to us being pastors of a local church. God will always do good to those who love Him and seek His will. God elevated me to heights I had never imagined possible, and it happened in the midst of Jezebel's most powerful reign. It seemed as though we were both reaching new heights at the same time.

I am aware that this woman, consumed by the Jezebel spirit, harbored a great affection for God. She enjoyed the higher stages of Glory, but she became disinterested at some point. I know it was because of the spirit in her that desired to be lifted up and delighted in the experience. The Church we had was in no way, shape, or form defunct. We had a huge gathering of hungry folks, and we were fortunate in that we were not turned away. Before I get into that aspect of ministry, allow me to take you back to the very beginning of the story.

We had a lot of difficulties in the beginning of the ministry, and I learned a lot during that time. First and foremost, we shall begin with our decision to enter full-time ministry. When we incorporated the ministry, she persuaded me that she should be the President and I should be the Vice-President, which I agreed to. She desired control, and she made use of her position to maintain that power.

Some may argue that I was simply the victim of a dominating wife. I want you to understand the distinction between a domineering wife and a Jezebel-like wife.... The domineering wife is exactly that: she is in charge. The Jezebel spirit employs witchcraft, control, deception, and familiar spirits in order to achieve her goals.

When the Ministry began to generate revenue, it was time to begin receiving compensation for the job performed by the Ministry. She persuaded me once more that, despite the fact that I was the one who traveled, spoke, and handled the day-to-day ministry, she should be the one who got compensated financially. As a result, she received a salary for four years while

JEZEBEL'S STRONGHOLD: THIS IS THE STORY OF AN ACTUAL MAN'S JOURNEY

I did not receive a single penny. You can argue that she was your wife, but.... Anyone who puts forth a lot of effort should be compensated. It's a slap in the face, to put it mildly. It wasn't until four years later that I earned a wage, and it was only half of what I had been earning since I started. For the duration of our marriage, I was required to send her my whole paycheck as soon as I received it. Jezebel is in complete command of the finances. Every decision had to be approved by her, and she was very strict about who could make what decisions.

One thing that I didn't notice until after I left was the number of folks who were in pain. If somebody got in Jezebel's way or seemed to be more attracted to me than she was, it was time to cut them loose. She would expel individuals from Church and even cut them off, and I'm sure it was upsetting to some people. After my eyes were opened to this reality, I sobbed uncontrollably for several minutes. No one should ever be denied the opportunity to receive from the Church. Every time I began to receive acknowledgment, she would cut them off, claiming that she should be the center of attention. Jezebel will always find a way to excuse all of the devastations they cause.

By the time we were ordained as pastors, she had developed into the most powerful woman. One thing that people did not realize they were doing was elevating Jezebel to the position of ultimate ruler. Everyone who saw her as she was or came close to her had a female presence around her at all times, and she had them affirming every hurt and devastation she had inflicted on anyone who witnessed her or came close to her. She was the hostess of numerous late-night gossip sessions. It had gotten to the point where if Jezebel said anything, it would be backed up by everyone or they would all be killed. She would sit in the sound booth, and soon there would be a crowd gathered around her to watch her. The manifestation of signs and marvels would take place throughout our encounters, and she would just glisten as she stared at them. She didn't want anyone else to have access to them but herself. The problem was that, at every gathering where the signs appeared, she would display them for everyone to see, and then the presence of God would fade away. God was no longer the focal point of the story. People continued to arrive night after night, and the meetings had never been better, and once Jezebel and I were ushered into the dining area, things became even better. I'd be told that she wasn't getting enough attention and that I'd messed up the meeting, among other things. Ninety percent of the time, something like this would take place. As soon as someone entered through the door, she would tell them to stay quiet. She didn't want anyone to see her true colors, so she hid them. She would sneer at me and pull out the signs and wonders that had occurred during the meeting, and then she would be surrounded by people who agreed with her that the meeting had been fantastic.

She reached a point when controlling my life was no longer enough, and she needed to control many others as well. People would be unable to make even the most fundamental decisions without her consent. One woman was barred from socializing with anyone because Jezebel had ordered her not to, and she was upset. I'm talking about people who were even a part of our Ministry team at one point. This woman was the final person who remained under her control after I had fled the country. (Please, God, assist her.)

Jezebel even managed to persuade the entire Church that we should pray for the destruction of another Church. There

JEZEBEL'S STRONGHOLD: THIS IS THE STORY OF AN ACTUAL MAN'S JOURNEY

was a Church that personally attacked me from within her own Ministry, but Jezebel held special prayer gatherings to prevent that Ministry from obtaining a building on which to operate. It doesn't matter how you look at it, this is witchcraft. This carried on for months and months. This was just one of a series of meetings held in opposition to something or someone.

This is exactly what someone who possesses the Jezebel Spirit does. They will begin at their residence and then proceed to the Church, where they will continue until they reach the top or demolish the Church, whichever comes first. Finally, the spirit will begin to spread its poison to other churches and cities throughout the world.

The Reign of Jezebel has come to an end

God had a plan to dethrone Jezebel after she had been elevated to the position of queen. At the time, I had spent hours praying and seeking the Lord's guidance regarding how I was feeling. As a result, I would be exalted up by the Lord and smashed by Jezebel. We were in the midst of a Revival that had lasted for two years without interruption. There were moments when I would pray to the Lord that when the Revival was over, I might simply depart and leave everyone pleased.

Approximately one month before I departed, God performed more miracles than he had ever performed before. People have been healed of cancers and have experienced other real miracles. It was fantastic, but it was also quite difficult in terms of my personal life. In a voice from the heavens, God instructed us to hold a special Cast-Out Devil's Conference on a Thursday night. I had no idea that the next weekend would be my final time in the city. The Cast-Out Devil's Conference might not seem like a compelling title for a conference, yet we were jam-packed with attendees. God had promised me that He would notify me when it was time to depart. Many people participated in the expulsion of devils on Thursday night. On that night, God anointed me to give demons the count of three and five in order for them to depart, and they did. On the ground, people were crawling like snakes because of the heat. Jezebel would attempt to incite people who had already been delivered, but she would fail miserably. Jezebel would try to stay near to me in order to give the impression that she was being used by God. At the conclusion of the meeting, Jezebel was standing in the aisle, and I approached her and asked if she needed anything, to which she said emphatically NO!!! It appeared to me that she had lost her last chance to maintain Revival. Jezebel was enraged after the meeting because God had anointed me in such a way that it moved the focus away from her and onto me.

God revealed to me that Saturday night would be the grand finale of my life. Friday night was fantastic, and it was one of the best meetings I've ever participated in, but it paled in contrast to Saturday night. On that particular night, there were more signs and wonders than at any other point in the revival's history. There were people who were hit with God's Glory on a completely different level.

We had a special guest speaker on Sunday, and the meeting was really tense. There was no anointing or movement of the Spirit. After the meeting, I began to express my dissatisfaction to Jezebel, saying that something didn't feel quite right. GOD IS GOING TO GO!!! I heard the nicest word for the Lord. How exciting! I knew I was leaving and told Jezebel that I would be departing shortly. She told me to have a few members of the team pray for me. As a result, I agreed to stay till the next day. Jezebel informed my own team that I wished to leave because I was possessed by demons, and she also persuaded them that I was leaving for another woman in the Church, which they believed. For hours, I was subjected to verbal assaults on my

JEZEBEL'S STRONGHOLD: THIS IS THE STORY OF AN ACTUAL MAN'S JOURNEY

decision to leave and about this other woman. See, there was no longer anything wrong with her, only with me and the other people around her. Once I had gotten some distance from them, I contacted the woman they were talking about and asked her if she would mind leaving with me, because I was leaving with or without her. She stated that if you go, I will go. She was the mother of two children, and the way these so-called Christians were acting would have terrified them for the rest of their lives. Finally, I dashed into my office, stuffed an empty box with clothes, and dashed out the door, Jezebel shouting that he was leaving behind him. Three ladies were racing after me as I ran down the corridor. As soon as I got into my old van, they jumped in to prevent me from driving away. They realized after a while that they were not going to be able to stop me. I walked out the door and swung around the corner to pick up the woman they were referring to before. Was this the perfect situation? Certainly not, but you don't know what you would do till you are chased by a group of Christians. As soon as we got in the car and drove away, my eyes were wide open. I was witness to everything Jezebel had done. The next thing we knew, we were being pursued by several automobiles. Yes, we were involved in a car chase with Jezebel. After a long period of time, we were able to get away. It was observed because of how it seemed, but I felt God had told me to go!!!

After we had departed, stories began to circulate, and I decided to leave the Ministry for another woman. The truth is that I and another woman were forced to leave Jezebel. After I had departed, I spoke with one of the women on my right-hand ministry team, and she admitted that my wife at the time was Jezebel out of her own mouth. Another woman from the ministry approached my vehicle and stated that everything that had been done against me was incorrect.

As you can see, Jezebel bribed members of the Church Team into praying witchcraft prayers against me and everyone else who had left. It was my departure that prompted Jezebel's rage to erupt, and she was exposing herself. After they had left, I was informed of the twenty-four-hour prayer to bring me back by a third party. The prayers included requests such as that I do not have any money and that relationships be severed, among other things. There was also a time when she said that Jezebel used salt and pepper to cast a spell on her. She had me dismissed two days after I had resigned from the Ministry of Health and Human Services. She created the impression that she wanted me back, but this was also a fabrication.

God foresaw the events that would lead to Jezebel's eruptive outburst and show her real colors. This marked the beginning of a period in which many people's eyes were opened. The Revival went on with great secrecy around my reasons for departing the group. They were informing others that I was experiencing a family emergency.

Lies, deception, and witchcraft were still being used. There were stories about me leaving the ministry and having affairs with a number of different women, all of which were unfounded. They tracked down my address and drove by it several times a day, praying against me in the process. I had, in fact, become Jezebel's adversary, as did everybody who dared to oppose her. The Revival did come to an end after Jezebel was caught up in the web of events. Many people believe I was responsible for Revival's demise, but the truth is that God decreed the Grand Finale. God brought it to an end that day and began the process

JEZEBEL'S STRONGHOLD: THIS IS THE STORY OF AN ACTUAL MAN'S JOURNEY

of dethroning Jezebel's Kingdom. It was necessary for me to lay down my life in order for her to fall.

I am well aware that I could have done things differently, but I did the right thing. In the days following my departure, I received a prophetic Word from a Prophet who told me that Jezebel was sucking the life from my veins. He told me that I had to go in order to survive. I spoke with a lawyer about the possibility of divorcing her. Because she was unwilling to change, I was forced to divorce the woman who was known as Jezebel. She wanted to be in charge of everything, including that. As a result, I released five autos, a ministry, and five homes after God ordered me not to fight for anything. She desired to be the one who initiated the divorce proceedings. So I gave her permission, and she filed in a separate county so that no one would know she had filed, and she received everything but one old van. She wished to preserve the impoverished woman who had been abandoned by her husband in favor of another woman. This was a front she wanted to maintain in order to gain compassion. Following my departure, the divorce was finalized roughly five weeks after I had departed.

The church where I used to worship has been demolished and is now an empty structure. I don't care about that portion, but I had hoped that, as the prophetic man of God, people would have listened to me instead of Jezebel in this situation.

Jezebel's characteristics are as follows

Listed below are a few of the qualities of Jezebel that this woman possessed. With a description of how she became infected, I shall outline the characteristics of the disease.

These individuals are on a mission to eliminate the true prophets and prevent them from assuming their proper position within the Church. (They despise the true prophet because they are afraid of being exposed.)

This woman was slowly but steadily taking my life. After my eyes were opened, I saw her for who she truly was, and I became her adversary. Because of God, she was unable to complete her mission of destroying me.

They are attempting to ascertain the position of the authentic prophet.

She was attempting to undermine my own position as the prophetic voice that the Church listened to and followed.

They agitate and manipulate the situation.

She was arousing the attention of everyone who was gathered around her. There was always an opponent of some sort, and she persuaded everyone who followed her to pray for that individual.

They are motivated by hatred, vengeance, and murder. (Destroying someone's reputation is included among the many definitions of murder.) That is exactly what Jezebel will attempt to do to people who have seen through their deception.

She would assassinate the reputation of anyone who attempted to leave the Church under her supervision. She did this in anticipation of my departure. She spread numerous stories, including the one that the lady she was accused of having an affair with was pregnant with my child. That woman has never been pregnant, let alone with my child, and this is still the case now.

They have a spirit of deception.

The act of stating anything that is false or inventing something that is not true is a lie. This woman was well-known for fabricating stories about other people.

They play games with their partner and manipulate him or her.

This was proven to be correct. She managed to persuade me on a consistent basis that what she did was always correct. If she wanted us to pray against another ministry, she had a way to persuade you to comply, and if you didn't, you were the next person on her hit list, which included me.

Jezebel employs the practice of witchcraft.

Witchcraft is the practice of praying for bad things to happen to other Christians. This woman has done this numerous times in the past toward anyone she regarded to be her adversary. It was brought to my attention by persons close to her that she had prayed specific prayers against me.

They have a strong sense of authority.

This meant she would have to be the one in charge of all choices made within the ministry. After that, she began to exert influence over members of the church, and eventually over her own mother, over whom she exercises authority over her income and decisions.

They do not act in accordance with what is right in God's eyes, but rather according to what is right in their own eyes.

She has the power to persuade others that what she was doing was correct, even though it was in direct opposition to God and His Word.

They accuse Authentic Prophets of not delivering the entire true Word of the Lord in its entirety.

In the event that a Prophet spoke something she didn't agree with, she would proceed to break the Words apart. Indeed, this was true of the words I spoke in the last month before I left the country. She was able to persuade everyone who remained that it was not the real Word of God.

Jezebel possesses a seductive spirit, and she infects the body of Christ in the same way that a virus infects a computer.

It reached to the point where everyone in the group became entangled in Jezebel's web of control. Some people were even unable to pay their payments without first consulting her with regard to them.

They are looking to be the focus of worship and/or the center of attention in their community.

She was in charge of the music and the worship service. She didn't want anyone to know who the songs were by and she didn't want them to know who she was. She would crank down the volume on all of the worship team's microphones so that hers was the loudest.

They are strict in their demands for compliance to their every command.

You had to show there if she phoned, or you'd be kicked from the team. If you didn't answer in a respectful manner, you were kicked off the team.

Jezebel prophesies through the assistance of familiar spirits.

She would converse with others and prophesy about things she had gathered from their interactions.

They are full of intimidation, pride, and hatred, and they refuse to submit (but appears to be submitted.) and they foment strife among the people.

All of this was true in the case of this woman. She was completely preoccupied with all of these things. There were times when she was intimidating to the point where you would believe something was wrong with you. She had such high

JEZEBEL'S STRONGHOLD: THIS IS THE STORY OF AN ACTUAL MAN'S JOURNEY

expectations of herself that she believed she could do no wrong. She was enraged by anyone who disavowed the Church or saw her for who she truly was. She would only acquiesce if she was in command and sowing strife in order to separate anyone who was closer to her than she was to anyone else. There were two women, and if they became close at any point, she would speak badly of one of them in order to separate them.

They are unable to admit they were incorrect. It's always the fault of someone else.

She never did anything wrong, and if you were under the impression that she did, she made you feel guilty.

Jezebel is attracted to individuals who are weak.

When we first met, I was a frail individual. She had a strong grip on people who were weak.

'Happily Ever After' is a fairy tale.

After allowing Jezebel to kill herself via her own nefarious schemes, we were finally able to enjoy our freedom. You have no idea how liberating it is to be free of such oppressive tyranny. I am now remarried to a great woman who is the mother of two daughters. Now I understand what it's like to be in a true marriage. It is a mutually beneficial partnership with God at the center of everything you do. I have a thriving ministry, and despite all of the lies she spread about me, everything is working out for the best. People have gently trickled in here and there to the meetings since it is true that you can tell who is who by their produce. It is becoming apparent to others that God has redeemed me, despite the fact that I departed in a contentious manner. Even if any of the reports were accurate, they appear to have lost sight of the incredible compassion of salvation and repentance available to them. God is so faithful that even when

Jezebel tries to kill you and turn the Church against you, He is always there to support you and protect you.

Also by Bill Vincent

Building a Prototype Church: Divine Strategies Released
Experience God's Love: By Revival Waves of Glory School of the Supernatural
Glory: Expanding God's Presence
Glory: Increasing God's Presence
Glory: Kingdom Presence of God
Glory: Pursuing God's Presence
Glory: Revival Presence of God
Rapture Revelations: Jesus Is Coming
The Prototype Church: Heaven's Strategies for Today's Church
The Secret Place of God's Power
Transitioning Into a Prototype Church: New Church Arising
Spiritual Warfare Made Simple
Aligning With God's Promises
A Closer Relationship With God
Armed for Battle: Spiritual Warfare Battle Commands
Breakthrough of Spiritual Strongholds
Desperate for God's Presence: Understanding Supernatural Atmospheres
Destroying the Jezebel Spirit: How to Overcome the Spirit Before It Destroys You!
Discerning Your Call of God

Glory: Expanding God's Presence: Discover How to Manifest God's Glory

Glory: Kingdom Presence Of God: Secrets to Becoming Ambassadors of Christ

Satan's Open Doors: Access Denied

Spiritual Warfare: The Complete Collection

The War for Spiritual Battles: Identify Satan's Strategies

Understanding Heaven's Court System: Explosive Life Changing Secrets

A Godly Shaking: Don't Create Waves

Faith: A Connection of God's Power

Global Warning: Prophetic Details Revealed

Overcoming Obstacles

Spiritual Leadership: Kingdom Foundation Principles

Glory: Revival Presence of God: Discover How to Release Revival Glory

Increasing Your Prophetic Gift: Developing a Pure Prophetic Flow

Millions of Churches: Why Is the World Going to Hell?

The Supernatural Realm: Discover Heaven's Secrets

The Unsearchable Riches of Christ: Chosen to be Sons of God

Deep Hunger: God Will Change Your Appetite Toward Him

Defeating the Demonic Realm

Glory: Increasing God's Presence: Discover New Waves of God's Glory

Growing In the Prophetic: Developing a Prophetic Voice

Healing After Divorce: Grace, Mercy and Remarriage

Love is Waiting

Awakening of Miracles: Personal Testimonies of God's Healing Power

Deception and Consequences Revealed: You Shall Know the Truth and the Truth Shall Set You Free
Overcoming the Power of Lust
Are You a Follower of Christ: Discover True Salvation
Cover Up and Save Yourself: Revealing Sexy is Not Sexy
Heaven's Court System: Bringing Justice for All
The Angry Fighter's Story: Harness the Fire Within
The Wrestler: The Pursuit of a Dream
Beginning the Courts of Heaven: Understanding the Basics
Breaking Curses: Legal Rights in the Courts of Heaven
Writing and Publishing a Book: Secrets of a Christian Author
How to Write a Book: Step by Step Guide
The Anointing: Fresh Oil of God's Presence
Spiritual Leadership: Kingdom Foundation Principles Second Edition
The Courts of Heaven: How to Present Your Case
The Jezebel Spirit: Tactics of Jezebel's Control
Heaven's Angels: The Nature and Ranking of Angels
Don't Know What to Do?: Discover Promotion in the Wilderness
Word of the Lord: Prophetic Word for 2020
The Coronavirus Prophecy
Increase Your Anointing: Discover the Supernatural
Apostolic Breakthrough: Birthing God's Purposes
The Healing Power of God: Releasing the Power of the Holy Spirit
The Secret Place of God's Power: Revelations of God's Word
The Rapture: Details of the Second Coming of Christ
Increase of Revelation and Restoration: Reveal, Recover & Restore

Restoration of the Soul: The Presence of God Changes Everything

Building a Prototype Church: The Church is in a Season of Profound of Change

Keys to Receiving Your Miracle: Miracles Happen Today

The Resurrection Power of God: Great Exploits of God

Transitioning to the Prototype Church: The Church is in a Season of Profound of Transition

Waves of Revival: Expect the Unexpected

The Stronghold of Jezebel: A True Story of a Man's Journey

Glory: Pursuing God's Presence: Revealing Secrets

Like a Mighty Rushing Wind

Steps to Revival

Supernatural Power

The Goodness of God

The Secret to Spiritual Strength

The Glorious Church's Birth: Understanding God's Plan For Our Lives

God's Presence Has a Profound Impact On Us

Spiritual Battles of the Mind: When All Hell Breaks Loose, Heaven Sends Help

A Godly Shaking Coming to the Church: Churches are Being Rerouted

Relationship with God in a New Way

The Spirit of God's Anointing: Using the Holy Spirit's Power in You

The Magnificent Church: God's Power Is Being Manifested

Miracles Are Awakened: Today is a Day of Miracles

Prepared to Fight: The Battle of Deliverance

The Journey of a Faithful: Adhering to the teachings of Jesus Christ

Ascension to the Top of Spiritual Mountains: Putting an End to Pain Cycles

After Divorce Recovery: When I Think of Grace, I Think of Mercy and Remarriage

A Greater Sense of God's Presence: Learn How to Make God's Glory Visible

Do Not Allow the Enemy to Steal: To a Crown of Righteousness, a Crown of Thorns

There Are Countless Churches: What is the Cause of Global Doom?

Creating a Model Church: The Church is Undergoing Considerable Upheaval

Developing Your Prophetic Ability: Creating a Flow of Pure Prophetic Intent

Christ's Limitless Riches Are Unsearchable: God Has Chosen Us to Be His Sons

Faith is a Link Between God's Might and Ours

Increasing the Presence of God: The Revival of the End-Times Is Approaching

Getting a Prophecy for Yourself: Unlocking Your Prophecies with Prophetic Keys

Getting Rid of the Jezebel Spirit: Before the Spirit Destroys You, Here's How to Overcome It!

Getting to Know Heaven's Court System: Secrets That Will Change Your Life

God's Resurrected Presence: Revival Glory is Being Released

God's Presence In His Kingdom: Secrets to Becoming Christ's Ambassadors

God's Healing Ability: The Holy Spirit's Power is Being Released

God's Power of Resurrection: God's Great Exploits

Heaven's Supreme Court: Providing Equal Justice for All
Increasing God's Presence in Our Lives: God's Glory Has Reached New Heights
Jezebel's Stronghold: This is the Story of an Actual Man's Journey
Making the Shift to the Model Church: The Church Is In the Midst of a Major Shift
Overcoming Lust's Influence: The Way to Victory
Pursuing God's Presence: Disclosing Information
The Plan to Take Over America: Restoring, We the People and the Power of God
Revelation and Restoration Are Increasing: The Process That Reveals, Recovers, and Restores
Burn In the Presence of the Lord
Revival Tidal Waves: Be Prepared for the Unexpected
Taking down the Demonic Realm: Curses and Revelations of Demonic Spirits
The Apocalypse: Details about Christ's Second Coming
The Hidden Resource of God's Power
The Open Doors of Satan: Access is Restricted
The Secrets to Getting Your Miracle
The Truth About Deception and Its Consequences
The Universal World: Discover the Mysteries of Heaven
Warning to the World: Details of Prophecies Have Been Revealed
Wonders and Significance: God's Glory in New Waves
Word of the Lord
Why Is There No Lasting Revival: It's Time For the Next Move of God
A Double New Beginning: A Prophetic Word, the Best Is Yet to Come

Your Most Productive Season Ever: The Anointing to Get Things Done

Break Free From Prison: No More Bondage for the Saints

Breaking Strongholds: Taking Steps to Freedom

Carrying the Glory of God: Igniting the End Time Revival

Breakthrough Over the Enemies Attack on Resources: An Angel Called Breakthrough

Days of Breakthrough: Your Time is Now

Empowered For the Unprecedented: Extraordinary Days Ahead

The Ultimate Guide to Self-Publishing: How to Write, Publish, and Promote Your Book for Free

The Art of Writing: A Comprehensive Guide to Crafting Your Masterpiece

The Non-Fiction Writer's Guide: Mastering Engaging Narratives

Spiritual Leadership (Large Print Edition): Kingdom Foundation Principles

Desperate for God's Presence (Large Print Edition): Understanding Supernatural Atmospheres

From Writer to Marketer: How to Successfully Promote Your Self-Published Book

Unleashing Your Inner Author: A Step-by-Step Guide to Crafting Your Own Bestseller

Becoming a YouTube Sensation: A Guide to Success

Watch for more at https://revivalwavesofgloryministries.com/.

About the Author

Bill Vincent is no stranger to understanding the power of God. Not only has he spent over twenty years as a Minister with a strong prophetic anointing, he is now also an Apostle and Author with Revival Waves of Glory Ministries in Litchfield, IL. Along with his wife, Tabitha, he, leads a team providing apostolic oversight in all aspects of ministry, including service, personal ministry and Godly character.

Bill offers a wide range of writings and teachings from deliverance, to experiencing presence of God and developing Apostolic cutting edge Church structure. Drawing on the power of the Holy Spirit through years of experience in Revival, Spiritual Sensitivity, and deliverance ministry, Bill now focuses mainly on pursuing the Presence of God and breaking the power of the devil off of people's lives.

His books 50 and counting has since helped many people to overcome the spirits and curses of Satan. For more information or to keep up with Bill's latest releases, please visit www.revivalwavesofgloryministries.com. To contact Bill, feel free to follow him on twitter @revivalwaves.

Read more at https://revivalwavesofgloryministries.com/.

About the Publisher

Accepting manuscripts in the most categories. We love to help people get their words available to the world.

Revival Waves of Glory focus is to provide more options to be published. We do traditional paperbacks, hardcovers, audio books and ebooks all over the world. A traditional royalty-based publisher that offers self-publishing options, Revival Waves provides a very author friendly and transparent publishing process, with President Bill Vincent involved in the full process of your book. Send us your manuscript and we will contact you as soon as possible.

Contact: Bill Vincent at rwgpublishing@yahoo.com

About the Publisher

Accepting manuscripts in the most categories. We love to help people get their words available to the world.

Revival Waves of Glory focus is to provide more options to be published. We do traditional paperbacks, hardcover, audio books and ebooks all over the world. A traditional royalty-based publisher that offers self-publishing options. Revival Waves provides a very author friendly and transparent publishing process, with President Bill Vincent involved in the full process of your book. Send us your manuscript and we will contact you as soon as possible.

Contact Bill Vincent at rwgpublishing@yahoo.com